A Realtor's Guide to Greater Success

Above and Beyond the Competition

Nancy D. (Hollandersky) Butler

DEDICATION

This book is dedicated to my mother, Bunny Hollandersky Stern, who died August 23, 2013.

Although we all have our share of difficulties in life, some of us have more than others, and my mother certainly had more than her share. Still, she maintained a positive attitude through it all and pushed on. She had a great will to live, and I am most proud of her attitude through it all.

Life is what you make it. And my mother sure was an inspiration to us all on perseverance and the pursuit of a happier life.

Mom, I miss you.

CONTENTS

INTRODUCTION

Like a lot of industries today, the real estate market is ever changing. This is true for buyers, sellers, realtors, and businesses that serve this industry.

In 2012, I interviewed realtors in different parts of the country to discover the greatest challenges to their career success. Was there a common thread among them all? Or were the challenges different based on region?

Regardless of location, their challenges were all basically the same. The same issues and frustrations kept them from the success they were striving for.

It was also interesting to find that what realtors loved about their careers was also much the same.

I have always said that many of us spend more of our waking hours in our careers than with our families, friends, or any other activity. Life is too short to go to work every day and not love what we do.

This book will help realtors more clearly understand and address business challenges in today's real estate market and how they can do a great job for their clients while improving the bottom line of their businesses and have more enjoyable and successful careers.

CHAPTER 1

WHAT IS YOUR PASSION? WHAT IS SUCCESS TO YOU?

❧

**If it were three years from now
and you were looking back to today,
what would your business need to
"look like" for you to feel really good
about the progress you have made?**

Knowing what "fires you up" and what makes you feel great about going to work every day is an important key to success.

Is success…
- the amount of money you make?
- how many sales you close?
- the amount of money you make in the amount of time you are willing to devote to your business?
- the challenge of "being the best" in your field?
- how many people you help?

Or is it something else?

When you enjoy what you do, it shows. People can tell whether you are excited about your work with them or just going through the motions. People like to work with happy, competent, and successful people. In a prospective client's eyes, the question may not only be "Who can do a good job for me?" The question also is "Whom do I enjoy working with?" "Who can communicate with me in a way that I not only understand but feel they are committed to whatever is needed to get the job done right?"

**This is your business.
You have the power to make it as successful as you want it to be.**

CHAPTER 2

LESSONS I LEARNED MY FIRST YEAR IN BUSINESS

To be able to do a great job for the client, I felt I needed to learn all the facts and features about the products and services I was offering while at the same time learning how to run a business. This was a daunting task.

When with prospective clients, I found myself talking constantly. I was afraid if I stopped talking they might ask me a question I couldn't answer. I finally realized it was okay not to have all the answers on the spot. Having the right questions for clients and then truly listening to what they had to say was extremely important for me to be able to do the best job both for clients and for my business. I realized that as long as I had a good knowledge of the basics of the products and services I was offering and answers to their questions within a reasonable period, that was fine.

Important lessons I learned:
- Be quiet and listen to the client.
- I don't have to have all the answers on the spot.

As a realtor, you should take the time to really get to know your clients, including their "must have" list as well as their "it would also be nice to have" list and to be their partner in finding the right home or in selling theirs at the best price. They need to know and feel that your company is there to do a great job for them.

The term "your company" applies even if you are an individual salesperson or broker. "Your company" need not mean you alone. It means you and whatever resources or assistance you use from others. For example, this can include an answering service to assure the client has access to "your company" even when you are not in. It can mean a staff member or business partner and so many other resources available to you to run a successful company and serve your clients well.

With that in mind, another lesson I learned was not to wait to hire help until I thought I could afford it. Many business owners wait until they feel they can afford to hire help, which for many is far too long. Don't wait. If you hire the right person, he or she will more than pay for himself or herself in a very short period. An employee can free you up to do the things that bring more money into the business. More on this subject later.

CHAPTER 3

THE CURRENT REAL ESTATE MARKET: THE NEW REALITY IN REALTY™

❧

The Results of My Interviews

Realtors, buyers, and sellers alike are paralyzed by their insecurities in the economy. Fear of buying and selling in real estate has never been more simultaneous. Real estate professionals see a variety of issues that could affect sales and profit:

- Fear of the economy
- An increase in bank requirements for loan qualifications
- Lower appraisal of properties
- Buyers and sellers feeling that they can use the Internet to shop and buy for themselves
- Slower processing of real estate transactions by financial institutions and appraisers
- Negative portrayal of the real estate market by media

Fear of the economy

Due to the recent volatile economic climate, there is an overall concern that job insecurity is causing potential clients to remain in their current residence.

An increase in bank requirements for loan qualifications

Not many years ago, it was fairly easy to qualify for a mortgage. Recently, financial institutions have implemented more stringent requirements for individuals and families to qualify. This can make it more difficult and in some cases impossible for some clients to purchase real estate.

Lower appraisal of properties

Realtors are finding the appraisal process previously accepted by financial institutions may not be accepted today. Sometimes when the buyer and seller agree on a price, the financial institution places a lower value on the property. This can cause the seller to back out of the sale.

Buyers and sellers feeling that they can use the Internet to shop and buy for themselves

Buyers and sellers now have the option of using the Internet as a low-cost way to purchase and sell real estate. And although this may not always be in their best interest, it is still an option some buyers and sellers choose in place of hiring a realtor to represent them.

Slower processing of real estate transactions by financial institutions and appraisers

Slower processing of transactions can cause several problems. It can not only cause realtors to wait a long time before they are compensated for their work but can also give buyers or sellers a chance to change their minds and back out of the sale.

Negative portrayal of the real estate market by media

Recently, the media portrayed the real estate market in a poor light. They have reported of an expected decline in real estate values. This can cause potential buyers to wait to make a purchase until after prices drop even lower, leaving the realtor with fewer prospective buyers to work with.

"A New Reality in Realty ™" means real estate professionals need to think outside the box about things they *can* control and maximize their Stand-Out Value™.

What Is *Stand-Out Value* ™? The unique services and expertise a professional provides causing him or her to stand out among peers as the provider of choice. Stand-Out Value™ provides mutually profitable client experiences.

**If you and your competition offer the same product
and the same knowledge, at the same price,
why should the client work with you?**

Realtors who can answer this question thrive regardless of the market.

Managing "The New Reality in Realty™" means finding ways to work with this new reality while doing a great job for your clients and your business. You need to become great at managing the success of your clients and your business, regardless of these factors.

The following pages will outline ideas and strategies to incorporate into your real estate business for greater success.

CHAPTER 4

EVALUATING THE COMPETITION

～

Set yourself apart. What are you saying to the public? Often you can learn from your competition—not by copying what they do, but to get ideas to make you stand out.

- What are you saying?
- What is your competition saying?

Check how your competition is advertising. When reviewing area newspapers, I found the eye-catching advertising shown below. What do you see in your competition's advertising? How does it compare with and stand out against yours?

Need to sell?

It's a no-brainer—buying vs. renting

Always going above and beyond for you

Need land?

**Buyers and Sellers Receive
Up to $3,000 toward closing costs,
when you buy or sell with _____**

We take trades

**Your home on YouTube.
Watch now on your mobile device.**

Need to buy?

Need to rent?

Senior Saver Advantage Program

Price protection guaranteed

#1 Office for closed sales in 2008, 2009, 2010, and 2011 in New London County (based on CTMLS statistics)

What our customers are saying:
"You state what you can deliver and deliver on what you promise"

Guaranteed advertising

What our customers are saying:
"Your greatest asset is your integrity"

Proud to be voted Connecticut's
"Best Real Estate Company" in the Commercial
Readers' Poll
2009, 2010, & 2011

If we can't sell it, we'll buy it.

Meeting your needs…
exceeding your expectations

CHAPTER 5

MARKETING

⤚

Does the Public Know *All* You Can Do?

Consider this story.

An attorney handled a new client's divorce. The attorney did a great job, and the client was very happy with the outcome. One year later, the attorney and former client ran into each other at a party.

After exchanging greetings, the attorney asked the client how she was doing. The client went on to tell the attorney that she was doing very well. She had started her own business, had her own registered trademark, and had incorporated her business. The attorney then realized that her divorce client never knew that she also handled business law, including incorporating and registered trademarks.

The attorney needed to change the way she ran her business to ensure that all existing and potential clients know all she is able to do for them. Even though they may not need all of her services today, it is important that she "plant the seed" so they will think of her when the need arises.

What can you do for people that they may not be aware of? Does the public know *everything* you can do for them?

Think about it. Do your current and potential clients know all you can do for them?

- Purchase a home
- Sell a home
- Purchase land
- Sell land
- Rent an apartment, condo, or home
- Rent commercial property
- Purchase commercial property
- Sell commercial property
- You take trades
- Assist with short sales

How can you assure they know all you can do so they come to you when your services are needed? It is quite simple.

- Develop a small brochure that you can hand out to all current, future, and past clients. You can also use this at trade shows, public speaking opportunities, and other marketing opportunities.

- Talk about all you do. When you are asked about your profession or when an opportunity arises to speak about what you do, do not say "I am a realtor." Develop a really good "elevator speech."

Stand Out As the Realtor of Choice: Your "Elevator Speech"

Many business owners have heard of the elevator speech, a short paragraph in which you define your niche, your unique corner of the market. As a realtor, how can you make yourself stand out from all the other realtors with *your* elevator speech? What makes you different/better? Be sure to make it clear that you are different from "the average realtor."

Think of it this way: If you and a stranger entered the elevator at the same time, what would you say to him or her to describe what you do and why he or she should work with you, so that by the time the elevator has stopped and the stranger walks out, you have piqued his or her interest in talking with you further?

After you determine what makes you different/better than other realtors, incorporate that information into your ten- to twenty-second elevator speech. Practice your speech until you know it by heart and can state it whenever the opportunity arises.

Low-Cost and No-Cost Marketing

What I did: I learned early on that getting in front of one client at a time would not build the business fast enough. It was imperative that I get in front of a lot of people quickly, but I had little money to spend on marketing and had just moved to a new area. I needed to "think outside the box" and find low-cost ways to get the public to know who I am and what I can do for them.

How I did it: I looked in the yellow pages of area telephone books and went to libraries in the area to look up local clubs and professional organizations. I then contacted them and offered, as a free public service, to be a speaker for their meetings. I provided a list of topics I was qualified to speak on as well as a copy of my biography. Today, fortunately, you can do most of this online.

What were the results? After about six months, I found myself speaking, on average, once a month to groups of ten to one hundred people. This enabled me to get in front of a lot of potential clients quickly and build my business at minimal cost to me.

You can also be a public speaker for professional, charitable, or religious organizations to which you, your family, friends, or clients belong. On which topics of interest to the public can you—as a realtor with expertise in your field—offer to speak? Don't overlook the obvious: selling and buying real estate.

Selling
- Low-cost improvements that can increase the value of your home
- Financing options
- How to prepare your home to sell
- Staging
- De-cluttering

Buying
- Checklist to better assure you make the right purchase
- Qualifying for a mortgage
- Finding a great deal
- Home inspection: What does it cost, and is it worth it? How to find the right company.

Make sure all local newspapers know when you will be speaking. You can probably do this through a free news release. The organization you are speaking for may appreciate the publicity. Ask the organization for permission, however, before submitting anything to the media.

Also, team up and market with your client. Have your seller post copies of a color flyer that you provide on all available bulletin boards at work, and at clubs and organizations he or she belongs to, with a message to "take one."

Local and online radio shows

Both local and online radio shows often look for qualified guests to have on their shows. When in your car or any other opportunity you have, listen to a variety of radio shows, even if they are not your type of program. Pay attention to which stations have a talk show where your expertise would be a good fit. Make note of the station, the time, and the title of the show and the name of the interviewer. Set up a system in your computer to track all the information.

Next, call each station and offer to be a guest on the show you have selected. Explain that you have listened to and like the show and would be a great fit as a guest. Have a list of appropriate topics ready to discuss with the interviewer or station representative. Also, have your schedulefor the next twelve months available to enable you to book a date before you hang up.

Local television

The strategy here is the same as for radio. It is easier to start with local television stations or local cable access shows.

After you have found appropriate shows, contact the station and ask how to connect with the interviewer. As with radio, call each station and offer to be a guest on the show you have selected. Explain that you have listened to and like the show and would be a great fit as a guest. Have a list of appropriate topics ready to discuss with the interviewer or the station representative. Also, have your schedule for the next twelve months to enable you to book a date before you hang up.

Important points to keep in mind before contacting radio or television stations

- Be aware of topics they have recently covered so you do not duplicate.
- Know their audience and choose subject matter that is suitable.

Helpful tips

- Ask what clothing works best for the show. For example, you might be told not to wear loud prints or very bright colors.

- Have every show you are on recorded either by the station or a friend. This serves two purposes. First, after the show, listen to or watch your segment of the show. We often do not come across as we think we do. Seeing and hearing yourself will enable you to make changes to continually improve your radio and television presence. Second, you can use the recording for future marketing purposes.

When I first appeared on radio and television, I was concerned that an interviewer might ask me a question on the air that I may not have a good answer to. So I devised a way to ensure the station would have a great show and both the interviewer and I would provide great content. After we agreed to the topic, I asked the interviewer if they would like me to provide them a list of questions to ask me on the show. I told the interviewer I would provide the questions in advance of the show so that we both be well prepared. I have never had a show decline this offer.

When you write the questions, state them in a way that makes the interviewer look and sound good. For example, instead of writing: "What can home owners do to help their home sell more quickly?" say, "I know there are many things homeowners can do to help their home sell more quickly, such as removing clutter. What else do you suggest?"

By having the questions agreed to in advance, you can not only assure a great show but put yourself at ease at the same time.

More Tips for Advertising on a Budget

There are many inexpensive ways for small businesses to market themselves. Below are a few more options that can help you get your name out to the public.

- Write a letter to the editors of your local newspapers and industry trade magazines. Be sure it does not appear to be a sales pitch. Give advice and thank them for including it in their publication.

- Hold an open house at your place of business. Give people a reason to drop by—food, an educational seminar, a networking event, a party to celebrate a milestone (e.g., marking ten years in business), a fund-raiser for a charity, a document-shredding service, to meet a celebrity, etc. I held one in the summer and had an ice cream truck come with free ice cream for everyone who attended.

- Get a business card from everyone you meet who has one. Send a letter saying that you enjoyed meeting them and ask them to contact you if they ever need your services. You might want to enclose a coupon for 10 percent off your commission or a flyer for an event that you will be having soon, and a business card.

- Maintain a database of all contacts, including the business cards noted above. List the date you first connected with them, where you connected with them, their names, addresses, e-mail addresses, telephone contacts, and any other important information. Use this list whenever you have an event to invite people to, whenever you have sold a home in a contact's area, or whenever you have some other similar event. Be sure to keep track of each contact you have had with each person in your database. This will assure you are connecting with each person an appropriate number of times and at the right intervals.

- Donate your product or service to a charity auction. This can get your name out and help a charity that has meaning to you. A realtor could donate any of the following services:
  - A free walk-through and written recommendations on low-cost improvements homeowners can make to improve the value of their property (or to improve salability)
  - A market analysis to provide the client an estimate of the price his or her home may sell for

- Attend charity auctions and make business purchases when appropriate. Not only will you have the opportunity to network with attendees, you may also find some great deals on items you can use for your business. For example, I have won at charity auctions $4,500 of newspaper advertising for $850, a $10,000 skybox to a show for fifty people for only $2,000, radio advertising, and much more. All the money went to charity, and I got a great deal!

- Create a personal name tag or pin with your company name and logo on it. Wear it at all meetings, networking events, conferences, and other activities where you want to have your name and business in front of prospective clients.

- Free advertising: I was listed in the newspaper approximately once a month for about twenty years at no cost to me. I did this in two ways: 1) I sent a news release anytime I attended a training, spoke at a conference, or did anything else that was newsworthy. 2) I offered to be a resource for reporters whenever they were writing on a topic that was in my area of expertise.

"Outside the Box" Ideas

Think outside the box regarding what you can offer that others don't so the client will want to work with you instead of your competition.

- Offer in your ads to pay for a moving truck rental up to a certain amount when someone buys or sells through you.

- Provide moving services, such as paying for a certain number of hours of packing or basic cleanup before moving in.

CHAPTER 6

TECHNOLOGY AND SOCIAL MEDIA

❧

Online Marketing

Technology is constantly changing and improving the efficiency, effectiveness, and success of businesses. Having a great online presence is important, but it has to be designed to engage your potential customer and not just to capture a lead. It is important to focus on the following:

- Consistency of "your brand"
- Strategies to produce quick engagement and response
- Your image and online presence for the long-term
- Cost-effectiveness regarding time and money
- Continual improvement and evolution of your online tools

E-marketing

- Send a monthly newsletter or white paper on topics your potential customers want to know more about:

- ° Current financing options
- ° Things they can do to shorten the closing process
- ° Ten tips to find the perfect house
- ° Ten tips to help your home sell more quickly
- Online services offer inexpensive and personalized, upscale e-cards. Consider sending an e-card to contacts in your database with messages like these:
  - ° "Just Listed" e-cards
  - ° "Just Sold" e-cards
- Banner ads can also attract clients' attention and get them to view your website.
- Be sure to include on your website any letters or notes from satisfied customers. Of course, you will want to get their permission first. If they prefer that you not use their name, ask to use first names and the first initials of last names only.

Social Media

Research appropriate low-cost or no-cost online services available to increase your social media presence, including Facebook, Twitter, LinkdIn and Pinterest.

You can also write a blog that provides great content for your followers. Online programs are available to help automate this process for you, such as "www.hootsuite.com" and others.

Technology is ever-changing and improving. Be sure to set time aside each quarter to keep up-to-date on what is working, what is not, and what is new that could help you do better.

Technology Training Needs: Determine the systems you need and assess what training is needed for you and for your staff.

Technology for Business Management

Systems to enable you to run your business more efficiently

- Sales – to track potential as well as closed sales
- Prospect database management – to assure you are connecting with every prospect as often as you should and when you should
- Marketing – to evaluate marketing opportunities and track your marketing budget as well as the outcome of each marketing strategy you implement
- Expenses – this software should enable you to know where you stand at any given time financially and enable you to print reports for income tax preparation
- Required estimated tax payments – to track required payments and assure you are making them on time and in the correct amount

- Model week/schedule management – to enable you to set and follow an efficient model week
- Document management – to provide an electronic filing system to manage all required paperwork

Your broker may have software available for you or may be able to recommend a good software program that has been used by other realtors.

Your Website

- What is different/better about yours?
- How does it stand out?
- Keep it up-to-date and fresh (not stagnant)
- Post regularly
  - ○ Upcoming events you are participating in
  - ○ Awards you have received
  - ○ Holiday thank-you to all

Researching Technology

- Be sure to find out what training and support is available to you through the technology supplier (e.g., if you purchase a Microsoft product, check out what Microsoft support is available to you.)
- Consider the cost for support now and over the long-term.

Comparing Software and Online Systems

Software advertised to make your professional life easier or better is everywhere, but not all software is created equally. Before you invest in new software or in any technology, ask your colleagues what they have had success with, and be sure to consider multiple options. Compare features, ease of use, and compatibility with software you already have, if necessary. You can use a table like the one below to compare different options side by side.

Name of program				
Type of program *				
Web address				
Price range				
Support services				
Other				

* Marketing, tracking, coaching, etc.

CHAPTER 7

SETTING YOURSELF APART (STAND-OUT VALUE™)

❧

"Right from the start, make it right and stand apart!"

What makes you a better choice than your competition? What makes you stand out?

- Why should the client work with you?
- How are you helping potential clients know they need you?
- How are you enabling the public to know who you are?
- How are you different/better than the competition?
- What do you do that other realtors do not do for their clients?
- How does your *service* make you stand out to your potential clients?
- What do your ads say to make you stand out to your potential clients?

- What do you do to go above and beyond what is expected?
- How are you making it easy for people to do business with you?
- Do you have a written business plan?

Your Stand-Out Value™ – Be the Realtor of Choice.

Provide options for how existing and potential clients can communicate with you.

Many people today are extremely busy balancing work, family, and life in general. It is imperative that you make it easy for them to do business with you.

Today's technology provides several options for connecting with prospective clients. Consider making all of the following options available so people can use what works best for them. Be sure all options are listed on business cards, advertising, and any other communication.

Traditional phone

- During normal business hours, clients should be able to speak to a person and not just leave a voice message.
- During non-business hours, an answering service is preferable over voice messaging. Either way, there needs to be a way potential clients can leave a message for you.

- Provide a toll-free number.

E-mail: Be sure to check and reply to your e-mail messages at least hourly during normal business hours (or have staff manage them for you).

Text: Be sure to check and reply to your text messages at least hourly during normal business hours (or have staff manage them for you).

Fax: This can work well for any paperwork that does not require an original signature.

Website: Provide all options to connect with you on the home page and every page of your website.

Traditional: Your mailing address as well as your physical office address should be listed on all correspondence and marketing pieces.

The easier it is for people to connect with you and the quicker you reply, the better reputation you may have and the greater the opportunity for referrals.

Communicate the way every client needs you to.

Pay close attention to your tone and the way you present yourself to each prospective client.

For example, consider an elderly couple that lived in their home most of their adult life. Due to physical limitations, they now need to move to a place they can more easily manage. For them, you would want to be extremely compassionate and understanding, and respectful of the home they are asking you to sell for them. It may be that they have not been able to properly maintain their home and it needs work before you can put it on the market. Think about how you can tactfully address that issue without hurting their feelings or offending them.

You could say something like this. "I can see why you have loved living in your home all these years. It has some wonderful features that will really help to attract buyers. I have a few suggestions on things we can do to better assure you get a great price for your home."

Another example: consider a busy young family that has little time to deal with selling their home, buying another, and moving their entire family. You need to assure them that you will do everything you can to make the best use of their time, every time you connect with them. Consider sending them an e-mail in advance of their appointment outlining what you plan to accomplish at the meeting, anything they should have discussed or prepared prior to the meeting, and an estimate of the amount of time they should set aside for this meeting.

Find out what he or she needs, prefers, and doesn't like. Then agree with the client up front on the way you will be working together.

If you know it is important for you to work with clients in a way they do *not* prefer, explain why and get agreement. You are the expert to best assure their success.

Be sure to keep track of each client's or prospective client's preferences.

"Do unto others as you want others to do unto you" does *not* apply here.

Instead: Do unto others as *they* want to be done to. Remember, just because *you* like it that way, it doesn't mean that *they* do.

This means that you need to work with clients the way *they* need you to work with them. You must be flexible in the way you interact with clients. Keep in mind the way you present yourself, how loudly/softly you speak, and your use of technology—how you connect and how often you connect.

What do your customers feel about their experience with you?

- Do they know you really care about them? Do they feel you have their best interest in mind at all times?
- Are they confident in your ability to accomplish what they need from you?
- Do they feel you are there to help and assist them in making good choices, not to sell them something?
- Do they know their opinion and input are important to you?
- Are you always with a smile, professionally dressed, neat, and organized?

- Are you on the same page regarding the fee and the service they will receive?
- Do you always do what you say you are going to do when you say you are going to do it?
- Can they count on you no matter what?
- Do they go to you first when they need a realtor?

What do you do to go above and beyond? How can you provide an "outside-the-box" level of service?

- Bring their favorite beverage when you pick them up to view properties.
- Use the information you know to show you care, such as a card or small gift if it is their birthday.
- Observe special hours for your best clients.
- Return calls within an established time frame (by you or staff).
- Provide helpful guidance—above and beyond what is expected.

What else can you think of that will set you apart?

What are other ways you can customize how you provide value and stand out in the public eye?

Think about it this way. With so many realtors for home buyers and sellers to choose from, why should they choose you? What makes you different/better? How can you step up your game to stand out from the competition?

One example might be to offer a free packet to all prospective sellers on their first meeting with you. The packet could include information about preparing the home for sale:

"Easy, low-cost steps to help sell your home":

- Clean all windows inside and out.
- Paint the front door (talk to me about the color).
- Power wash the outside of your home if needed.
- De-clutter inside and out.
- De-personalize (e.g., remove photos).
- Put bright lightbulbs in every socket and lamp.
- Repair any wall holes.
- Touch up paint as needed.
- Complete any minor repairs, such as drippy faucets, loose handles, squeaky doors, and drawers that don't slide well.

You can also include a "to do" checklist to help with the sale and the move. Add to this list any other tips you have in this category.

- Another example of a free packet to provide all prospective buyers or sellers could include a list of service providers with whom you have a joint referral agreement. Think about who can help before the sale to get the house in order and who can help after the sale for any work that may be needed for the new resident.

Be sure to list a few in each category.

- Handyman
- Painter
- Electrician
- Plumber
- Landscaper
- Snow removal service
- Lawn care service
- Real estate attorneys
- Real estate lenders
- Movers
- Packing/shipping companies
- Places to drop off unwanted items and receive a receipt for tax purposes (e.g., Goodwill, Salvation Army)
- Places that will pick up unwanted items and give a receipt for tax purposes (e.g., Salvation Army, etc.)

IMPORTANT: Connect with all service providers before putting them on your list to assure they are the right people for you to recommend and that they will refer potential clients to you as well. They can also provide accurate contact and service information for you to include on your list.

Update your list whenever you receive a complaint or find another great resource.

What do you do to show your appreciation for your clients' business *after* the closing?

After the closing, give a packet to *your* buyer *and* to *your* seller, and one to the person who referred them to you.

Consider including the following:

- A handwritten thank-you note (this is better than an e-mail)
- Photo of their new home (it is even better if you can get a photo of the buyers in front of their new home)
- Incentive coupons for referrals
- A small gift with your logo on it—logo should not be too prominent.
- Fruit basket or flowers
- Lottery tickets
- Local movie tickets
- A brochure offering to speak as a free service to any organizations they belong to, their church or synagogue, or the charitable organizations they support. Include a sample of speaking topics, such as these:
    - Financing options
    - How to prepare your home to sell
    - Insight into how to assure the right purchase

CHAPTER 8

HIRING YOUR FIRST STAFF MEMBER

∽

As a coach to business owners in different parts of the country, I recommend a few important points when hiring your first staff member.

Many business owners wait to hire help until they feel they can afford to do so, which for many is far too long. Don't wait. If you hire the right person, he or she will more than pay for himself or herself in a very short period, which can free you up to do the things that bring more money into the business.

Think of it this way: Do you pay your attorney for his or her services at the same rate you pay for the work the attorney's paralegal or other staff members complete on your behalf? The answer is *no*. The attorney's time and expertise warrants a higher fee, as does your time and expertise.

As the business owner, you should not be spending your time doing work that you can hire others to do when they may not only be better at it, but can also do it at a lower cost to the business. You should be spending all of your time bringing in business to your company and managing the company, enabling the business to become more profitable.

Consider the following tasks for you and your assistant(s).

The realtor should focus on the following activities:
- Sitting with clients and prospective clients
- Showing properties
- Determining marketing strategies to implement
- Conducting the marketing strategies
- Strategizing better ways to serve clients, bring new clients in, and thank clients for their business
- Researching (only the research your staff cannot do for you)
- Working with staff to develop, implement, and monitor systems to ensure the business runs efficiently
- Continuing education

The assistant should focus on the following activities:
- Pulling together the marketing strategies the realtor has decided on
- Answering telephones
- Scheduling appointments
- Completing paperwork

- Preparing for meetings
- Managing office supplies
- Paying bills
- Researching
- Tracking expenses
- Tracking continuing education and license renewal requirements

The first time you hire, don't do it alone.

Many business owners are great at the business they are in but are not good at knowing how to hire the right person for their business. Get help from an expert.

1. Start by writing down the tasks you need the new hire to do. What should he or she be doing to help take your business to the next level? How many hours a week do you need him or her? Be clear on the personality traits you need in the new hire, such as enjoying working with people, being self-motivated and organized, etc.

2. Next, contact a temporary employment agency. Discuss what you need, and find out the following: What is the hourly rate charged to you for this employee? Of the amount charged to you, what hourly rate will the employee receive? Are you able to hire the employee initially as a "temp" through the agency and after three months sever the contract

and hire him or her as your own employee at no additional cost to you?

3. Finally, if the answer to the questions outlined in number two above are favorable, hire this agency to assist you. Staffing agencies are beneficial for many reasons:

   ○ They will go through many resumes and send you only the ones that appear to be a good fit for what you need.

   ○ The agency will guide you on fair compensation for that position.

   ○ For the first three months, the temp will not be your employee, so if at any time you feel the person is not working out, you can notify the agency, and it will find you someone else. You will not need to fire anyone.

   ○ You will not have to deal with payroll, tax reporting, employee benefits, or any of the required "payroll issues" until you know the employee is who you want and he or she becomes your employee.

   ○ Since you know what the employee is earning through the service, once he or she becomes your employee, you have "wiggle room" to increase the employee's pay when appropriate since you no longer have the employment service's fee to pay.

Also remember this: hire for personality, and train for skill.

You cannot change who a person is, his or her work ethic, or the person's ability. What you can change is a person's knowledge of what you need him or her to do and how you need him or her to do it for your business to be more successful. Personality can be more important than educational background and prior experience.

I often preferred to hire people who had never done the job I was hiring them for. That way I didn't have to "un-train" them before training them to do what I needed them to do.

Hire people because they have a great personality, the ability to learn quickly, and the desire to learn and do well. If they have that, you can train them to do almost anything.

CHAPTER 9

FOR THE REALTY COMPANY

❦

Why Should Agents and Brokers Be Affiliated with You?

The same issues apply here as outlined in the previous chapters of this book. Real estate companies can change the thought process so the agents or brokers are your clients rather than people looking to buy or sell property, since many of the same strategies apply.

What makes your firm stand out from all the other choices realtors have today?

- Do you have a system in place to provide greater education and guidance?
- Do you have a good training program?
- Are your affiliated costs competitive with or better than your competition?
- Do you have systems available to your realtors that allow them to "plug in and play" to make it easy for them to be successful?

- Do you provide one-on-one coaching when needed?
- Do you assist realtors with marketing?
- Do you bring in great speakers to your meetings to help realtors to think differently about their business?
- Do you provide office coverage options or ideas for realtors when they need time off?

Many real estate companies feel they are "the firm" to be affiliated with. What makes your firm a better choice than the competition to attract the best realtors to your firm, help them succeed, and keep them with you?

Review the other chapters in this book for ideas to help you stand out as the company of choice for the realtors you want to attract.

CHAPTER 10

BALANCING LIFE AND BUSINESS

❧

Taking Control of Your Business

Your model week

One key to maintaining a balance between business and your personal life is to manage and schedule your time effectively. Having a "model week" can be extremely helpful in assuring you allocate the right amount of attention to each area of your life.

When I first learned about a model week, I did not want anything to do with it. I felt it was more important that I was available to respond to whatever came up at work at the time it happened. That was until I realized I was wrong.

Having a model week can help you to not only be more efficient with your time but also be "present" with those around you and the work you are doing. Think about it this way. I would often take a call when I was in the middle of completing important paperwork. After I hung up the phone, it took me a very long time to get back to the mindset and place where I had left off, and therefore it took a lot longer to finish what I had started than if I had completed it from start to finish without an interruption.

Having a model week enables you to focus uninterrupted on what you are doing, and can enable you to do a better job and have quality time with everyone you interact with. This can be true at work as well as in your personal life.

Organize your work schedule to enable you to work efficiently and effectively and to truly have personal days.

Divide your week into three types of days:
- Focus days
- Buffer days
- Personal days

Each day is described as a twenty-four-hour period in which at least 80 percent of your waking time is spent on the tasks for that type of day.

Focus days

These days actually provide income to your business:
- Showing properties
- Conducting office appointments

- Calling current and prospective clients
- Marketing—conducting the event (not working on it)

Enter your focus days into your model week schedule after determining the following:

- How many focus days you will have per week
- How many appointments you will have per day
- How much time you will allow for each appointment

Buffer days

These days allow time to manage all the "stuff" that needs to get done in running your business:

- Paperwork
- Education, CEUs, reading, meetings
- Business planning
- Meeting with manager, broker, staff and other support people
- Marketing—planning
- Taking/returning phone calls
- Reviewing your tracking system to assure all work is completed on time
- Assessing and implementing the priority order to address your workload

Determine how many buffer days per week you will have. Then enter them into your model week schedule.

Personal days

On these days, you are completely free from work.
- No work of any kind
- Time with family and/or friends
- Alone time
- Vacation
- Personal appointments

Determine how many personal days per week you will have. Then enter them into your model week schedule.

Review the model week outline in the back of this book. Edit the shell to fit your needs and provide a copy to your staff so they know when they can book appointments for you. Monitor your system monthly, and make any adjustments needed.

When you first set up this system, you may need more buffer days until you become more efficient. You should work toward having mostly focus and personal days with fewer buffer days. This can happen when you are truly "present" for each type of day, you have fewer interruptions, and you have become better at delegating. If you are not good at sticking to your model week, assign a staff person or someone else to hold you accountable. If you do not have the right number of staff to help you, now is the time to evaluate making changes in that area.

Also, today many realtors are teaming up. This enables them to truly have a day or even a week or two off because they have someone they trust to cover for them.

Consider whether teaming up with a realtor you trust would be a good option for you.

Note: it may take a few weeks to be fully on track with your model week schedule.

CHAPTER 11

MONEY-SAVING TIPS AND BUSINESS CONFERENCES

❧

Money-Saving Tips

After researching credit card options, I put all of the business expenses I could on a credit card that provided two advantages: 1) Points for each dollar charged that could be used for a variety of other purchases. I would use the points to buy airline tickets, a gift for staff, or supplies. 2) Gave a statement that broke down all spending for the year by category—making tracking and income tax time much easier. Since the credit card was paid in full each month, the interest rate on the card was not an issue.

Should you attend a business conference?

As a small business owner myself, I attend at least one major conference each year. It is great to have an opportunity to connect with many other business owners face-to-face, rather than through the use of technology. It is a great opportunity not only to learn from the speakers but to network and get tips and ideas from others who do what you do. Also, many business owners find it difficult to break away and spend the time needed to focus on the changes necessary to "take the business to the next level." When at the office, it is easy to work through lunch, take calls, and do everything else that comes up, rather than taking time to focus *on* the business and not just working *in* the business. Attending a conference can "force" you to step away and focus and can inspire you to make the changes necessary for you to become more successful.

How to gain maximum benefit from attending a conference.

Many people have a tendency, when attending a conference, to sit in meetings and at meals with others they know. I suggest you do the opposite. Take advantage of the opportunity to network with the large number of people you have never met. By not sitting with anyone you know and not sitting with the same person more than once, you can connect with a large number of people and obtain many great ideas. Come to the conference with an open mind, and bring information you can share to help others. People are more willing to share great information with you when you share with them. By the end of the conference, you can meet and learn from so many people and help them as well.

Attend with the right attitude, and plan to come away with two or three strategies you will implement immediately to make a positive difference in your business. If you come away with concrete information to improve your business, your time and money will have been well spent.

CHAPTER 12

A NEW REALITY IN REALTY™: KEYS TO SUCCESS

‿

Start putting your plan into place now.

Review the steps outlined in this book that you have control over and can implement to put your business on track within the guidelines of *what success means to you.*

Taking control of your business. How many hours per week will you commit to making your business what you want it to be? Is the number of hours realistic for what you want to accomplish? If not, what should you adjust? Do you need to:

- º Devote more time to your business?
- º Change your business goals?
- º Hire more staff?

Take time now to write an outline that includes the following:

- The number of *hours* per week you will spend on your realty career
- The *opportunities* discussed in this book you will implement within the next six to twelve months
- The amount of *money* you will commit to advertising and other opportunities to promote your business
- Your *goals* for this year, including the amount of gross sales, and gross sales for last year in comparison

Review all material with your broker before using it.

- The broker can help assure it is appropriate and also give feedback on how to make it more effective.
- A second pair of "professional eyes" may cost you little to nothing and can help eliminate costly errors.

The business plan template on the following pages is available for you to download and edit for your use by completing the contact form located at: http://aboveallelse.org/speak-with-nancy/.

Be sure to request in the "message box" on this form to have the "Real Estate Business Plan Template" sent to you via e-mail.

BUSINESS PLAN

_____

DATE

_____

NAME OF BUSINESS

Mission statement: Many companies have a brief mission statement, usually thirty words or fewer, explaining their reason for being and their guiding principles.

Your "elevator speech": If you and a stranger entered the elevator at the same time, what would you say to him or her to describe what you do and why he or she should work with you, so that by the time the elevator has stopped you have piqued this person's interest to want to talk to you more?

Most important strengths and core competencies: What factors will make the company succeed? What are your major competitive strengths? What strengths do you personally bring to the business?

Significant challenges you face now and in the near future: What are your major competitive weaknesses?

What challenges do you have personally that may keep your business from succeeding?

Products and services: List your products and services, i.e., residential or commercial land and home sales, residential or commercial rental, buyer representative service, etc.

Marketing Plan

Important:

1. Put both your short- and long-term marketing plan in place now. The short-term plan involves planning where your clients will come from for the next three to twelve months. Long-term plans determine where your clients come from for the next one- to three-year period and after.

2. Branding yourself is important. Create your "brand." This is a certain "look," which includes color schemes, fonts, certain types of pictures or illustrations, etc. Use that same style on everything you publish, including your website and e-mail address, on all marketing pieces, and anything you give away. Consider including a picture of yourself. You may need to get each communication approved by your broker. But once the first one is approved, it should be easier and quicker to get it done each time thereafter.

3. There are many ways to market and build a following. It is important to track your marketing efforts. Different methods work in different markets. You want to discover quickly which marketing strategies pay off for you and which don't. You can either ask callers where they got your name and number from or use a system that captures this information for you. For example, implementing an automated "call-capture" system will enable you to know where the caller heard about your listing. You will need two different "tracks to run on": one that consists of all the

leads you want to continue to maintain and market to and one that consists of the different marketing strategies you will continue to employ. If you do not already have a good system in place, consider purchasing software to enable efficient ongoing tracking, monitoring, and marketing.

Standing out from the competition

See what others offer and how they advertise.

Check all local newspapers and note what other realtors are saying in their ads

- "Senior-Saver Advantage Program"
- We pay sellers' attorney fees
- Guaranteed advertising
- Price protection guaranteed
- Always going above and beyond for you
- It's a no-brainer—buying vs. renting
- #1 Office for closed sales in 2008, 2009, 2010, and 2011 in NL County (based on CTMLS statistics)
- "Meeting your needs…exceeding your expectations"
- Your home on YouTube (watch now on your mobile device)
- Buyers and sellers up to $3,000 toward closing costs when you buy or sell with __(name), or __(name)
- We take trades

- Proud to be voted Connecticut's "Best Real Estate Company" in the Commercial Readers' Poll 2009, 2010, and 2011

Does the public know all you can do? Do they know you can help them:

- Purchase land
- Sell land
- Rent an apartment, condo, or home
- Rent commercial property
- Buy a home
- Sell a home
- Buy commercial property
- Sell commercial property
- You take trades
- Assist with short sales

List everything you are able to do, even if it is not an area you typically focus on.

How are you different/better than the competition? What makes you stand out?

What do your ads say that make you stand out from the competition?

Define your niche: Based on the information noted here, you should have a clear picture of where your company best fits. In one short paragraph, define your niche, your unique corner of the market.

Review the "Realtor Marketing Overview" included in this book. Use the marketing strategies you already have as well as the opportunities in this book to write your short-term and long-term marketing plan here.

Include the following:

- Which strategies you will use
- When you will implement them
- The cost for each
- How you will track each
- The results you expect from each

BUDGET

	Last 12 Months Actual	Next 12 Months Planned
Operational		
Open houses		
Office expenses		
Gas		
Entertainment		
Advertising (newspaper, television, radio)		
Education		
Realtor.com		
Marketing services		
Signage		
Promotional material (e.g., postcards)		
Marketing miscellaneous		
Gifts		
Photography		

	Last 12 Months Actual	Next 12 Months Planned
Home staging		
Association fees		
Technology expenses		
Errors & omissions insurance		
Assoc. of Realtors dues		
License renewal		
Chamber of Commerce & other organizations		
Subtotal		
Grand Total		

Tracking

Set up and maintain a system to track all marketing and leads. Outline the strategies you will employ, including how and when you will have each in place:

- Type
- Frequency
- Expected views
- Cost
- Number of leads received

Commission Pricing

- What is your commission pricing strategy? Compare your commission structure with that of your competition.
- What can/will you offer regarding discount coupons and referral incentives?

Broker's Payout Structure

List here the payout structure offered by your broker. At least quarterly, monitor where you stand in comparison to the payout level just below and just above your current payout level. This can help to better assure you do not miss a higher payout rate that you could easily qualify for if you knew you had to do a little more to reach it.

Client Service

Have a printed handout at the first interview with prospective clients or when clients sign up. Go over it with them (do not just give it to them), including these aspects:

Home Buyers'/Sellers' Packets

- Easy steps to help sell your home
  - ○ Clean windows
  - ○ Paint front door
  - ○ Power wash if needed
  - ○ De-clutter inside and out
  - ○ Bright lightbulbs in every socket
  - ○ Repair wall holes
  - ○ Touch up paint
  - ○ De-personalize

- List of service providers that you have a joint referral agreement with
  - ○ Handyman
  - ○ Painter
  - ○ Electrician
  - ○ Plumber
  - ○ Landscaper
  - ○ Snow removal
  - ○ Lawn care

- º Real estate attorneys
- º Real estate lenders
- º Movers
- º Packing/shipping companies
- º Places that will pick up unwanted items and give a receipt for tax purposes (Bear that Cares, Salvation Army, etc.)
- º Places to drop off unwanted items (e.g., Goodwill, Salvation Army, etc.)

How Will You Show Your Appreciation for Their Business—After the Sale?

Will you give a packet after the closing to the buyer, the seller, and the person who referred them? What will you include?

- A handwritten thank-you note
- Photo of the buyer's new home
- Incentive coupons for referrals
- Gift—with your logo on it (not too prominently)
- Fruit basket
- Flowers
- Brochure offering to speak to organizations they belong to, including a sample of speaking topics such as:
  - Financing options
  - How to prepare your home to sell
  - Checklist to assure the right purchase

Will you give a gift (as allowed) to the person who referred you, value not to exceed the amount allowed by your firm? List here all gifts you will use and include the cost for each.

Technology and Social Media

Online Marketing

Technology is constantly changing and, for the most part, has improved ways to help a business be efficient, effective, and successful. Having a great online presence is important, but it has to be designed to engage your potential customer and not just to capture a lead.

Your business should focus on:

- Strategies to produce quick engagement and response
- Your image and online presence for the longterm
- Cost-effectiveness regarding time and money
- Continual improvement and evolution of your online tools

List your online marketing plan here.

Consider the following:

Social media; free web presence

- LinkedIn
- Facebook

- Twitter
- Pinterest
- A blog

Online programs can help automate this process for you, such as www.hootsuite.com and others.

E-marketing

- Your monthly newsletter or white paper
- "Just Listed" e-cards
- "Just Sold" e-cards
- Banner ads

Your website

Keep your website up-to-date and fresh (not stagnant).

Technology

Business-management systems to address the following:

- Sales
- Prospect contact
- Marketing
- Expenses
- Required estimated tax payments
- Model week/schedule management
- Document management
- Prospect database management
- Inventory management

Which software and online systems are you considering?

Comparing software and online systems:

Name of program				
Type of program*				
Web address				
Price range				
Other				

* Marketing, tracking, coaching, etc.

Technology Training Needed

After you determine the systems you will employ to assist in managing your business, you will then need to assess what training is needed for you and your staff to maximize use efficiently and effectively. When researching technology, be sure to find out the training and support that is available to you through them and what the cost would be. This information can help you decide which program would work best for you.

Sales Forecast

Prepare a quarterly projection for the next twelve months. Base the forecast on your historical sales, the marketing strategies that you have just described, your budget, and other factors outlined in this document.

You may want to do two forecasts as noted below. Keep notes on your research and your assumptions as you build this sales forecast. Relate the forecast to your sales history, explaining the major differences between past and projected sales.

- Low estimate that you are confident you can reach no matter what happens
- Your actual goal for the next twelve months that this plan supports

Operational Plan and Continuing Education

Operational Plan

- Where will you meet with clients?
- What are your business hours?

Legal Environment

Describe the following and associated costs:
- Licensing and bonding requirements
- Special regulations covering your industry or profession
- Insurance coverage—e.g., E&O

Continuing Education

- What is the requirement, and when is it due? List the resources available to you to fulfill the requirement, such as local or online schools, online training, etc. Keep this list up-to-date, including contact information.

Write your plan to ensure you are compliant with all of the above, not only on time but in advance of the deadline? This will remove stress and assure compliance in the event of unexpected roadblocks in your life or if business causes delays.

Staff and/or Partner

Partner - Consider whether having a business partner is appropriate for you. The goal may be to have someone in the office to

- cover for you during personal or vacation time off.
- cover for you when you are ill.
- share ideas and help each other to grow the business.
- share business expenses.

Answer these questions:

- What is your strategy to find the right partner and integrate each other into the business?
- What is your time line to have this in place?
- What do you need to know regarding any requirements or paperwork your broker, E&O insurance carrier, landlord, etc., requires?

Staff

What are your current and planned staff needs for the next year?

- Number of employees
- Type of labor (skilled, unskilled, professional)
- What will their pay structure be?

- What training methods, resources and requirements will you use?
- Who does which tasks?
- What is your schedule and theirs?
- Do you use contract workers as well as employees?
- If new employees will be needed in the coming year, how will you
  - locate them?
  - train them?
  - pay them?
  - assign hours of work?

How will you build client relationships based on trust, confidence, and loyalty?

- Customize "value propositions" for clients to select you as the realtor of choice.
- Develop and maintain your desired image.
- Define and build the experience you want for your clients.
- Increase referrals for future business.

Financial Goals

Cash Flow

Based on this business plan, what are your projections for this year and goals for the next three years?

Year One Expected Results

- Gross business income
- Total expenses
- Net profit

Year Two Planned

- Gross business income
- Total expenses
- Net profit

Year Three Planned

- Gross business income
- Total expenses
- Net profit

Year Four Planned

- Gross business income
- Total expenses
- Net profit

Staffing Goals

List the number of full-time and part-time staff and what their main functions will be.

Year One
Full Time: _____
Duties:

Part Time: _____
Duties:

Year Two
Full Time: _____
Duties:

Part Time: _____
Duties:

Year Three
Full Time: _____
Duties:

Part Time: _____
Duties:

Year Four
Full Time: _____
Duties:

Part Time: _____
Duties:

Time Management

MODEL WEEK Organize your work schedule to enable you to work efficiently and effectively and to enable you to truly have personal days.

	Sun	Mon	Tue	Wed	Thu	Fri	Sat
Focus, Buffer, or Personal							
7:00– 7:30							
7:30– 8:00							
8:00– 8:30							
8:30– 9:00							
9:00– 9:30							
9:30– 10:00							
10:00– 10:30							
10:30– 11:00							

	Sun	Mon	Tue	Wed	Thu	Fri	Sat
11:00–11:30							
11:30–12:00							
12:00–12:30							
12:30–1:00							
1:00–1:30							
1:30–2:00							
2:00–2:30							
2:30–3:00							
3:00–3:30							
3:30–4:00							
4:00–4:30							
4:30–5:00							

	Sun	Mon	Tue	Wed	Thu	Fri	Sat
5:00–5:30							
5:30–6:00							
6:00–6:30							
6:30–7:00							
7:00–7:30							
7:30–8:00							
8:00–8:30							

Use the codes below to fill in your model week chart.

CLM = Client meeting

A = Return calls

B = Client meeting prep

C = Marketing

D = Staff, partner, broker, CE classes, or other business meetings

E = Mail, research, finish up work after client leaves, e-mail, break, technology, etc.

Edit tasks and coding to fit your schedule.

Appendices

Include details and studies used in your business plan:

- Brochures and advertising materials
- Detailed lists of equipment owned or to be purchased
- Copies of leases and contracts
- List of marketing opportunities available
- Model Week instructions
- Any other materials needed to support the assumptions in this plan

REMEMBER

DON'T BE AFRAID TO TAKE CALCULATED RISKS.
IT MAY BE SCARY.
BUT WHEN YOU SEE SUCCESS,
IT IS INVIGORATING!

THIS IS ME LYING DOWN WITH A LIVE, FULLY
GROWN CHEETAH IN SOUTH AFRICA IN
MARCH 2013.

ABOUT THE AUTHOR

Nancy managed apartment complexes throughout Connecticut for eight years. She was managing approximately one thousand apartment units when she changed careers.

While in the process of a divorce, Nancy took her children and, with no child support, alimony, or other source of income, moved seventy miles away and started her own financial-planning and asset-management business. She built the business from scratch to approximately $200 million in assets under management and 1,200 clients. After twenty-five years, Nancy sold her practice and became a national speaker and consultant to help business owners do a better job for their clients and improve their bottom line. In 2012, she focused on helping realtors.

Nancy also speaks on topics to help individuals live a successful life and realize their dreams and to balance a successful business with a successful personal life.

Her first book *Above All Else, Success in Life and Business* was published September 2012.

Nancy has been quoted in many local and national publications, including *USA Today*, *Money Magazine*, and *The Day*, and has been a speaker for major corporations such as Pfizer, General Dynamics, and Dow Chemical, to name a few. Nancy has also been a guest on several live television and radio shows.

Nancy D. (Hollandersky) Butler
Above All Else, Success in Life and Business®
A division of Butler Communication LLC.
860-444-0535
www.aboveallelse.org
nbutler@aboveallelse.org